HANDS-ON HISTORY

PROJECTS ABOUT

Ancient China

Ruth Bjorklund

Marshall Cavendish
Benchmark

New York

For fellow adventurers: Neil, Denise, Kobe, Arie, and Thea

Benchmark Books
Marshall Cavendish
99 White Plains Road
Tarrytown, NY 10591-9001
www.marshallcavendish.us

Library of Congress Cataloging-in-Publication Data
Bjorklund, Ruth.
Projects about ancient China / by Ruth Bjorklund.
p. cm.—(Hands-on history)
Summary: "Includes social studies projects taken from the ancient Chinese"—Provided by publisher.
Includes bibliographical references and index.
ISBN-13: 978-0-7614-2257-0
ISBN-10: 0-7614-2257-9
1. China—History—Juvenile literature. I. Title. II. Series.
DS736.B57 2006
931—dc22
          2006002813

Title page: A section of the Great Wall of China, northwest of Beijing.

Maps by XNR Productions
Illustrations by Rodica Prato
Photo research by Joan Meisel

Photo credits: *Alamy*: 26, Ron Yue; 34, Alan King; *Art Resource*, NY: 8, *Giraudon*; 20, Snark; *Corbis*: 32, Royalty-Free; *Getty Images*: 22; *North Wind Picture Archives*: 6, 38; *Photo Researchers, Inc.*: 1, Rafael Macia; *The Bridgeman Art Library*: 4, *The Makins Collection*.

Printed in China

1 3 5 6 4 2

Contents

The Chinese were one of the first people to practice farming.
The invention of the foot-powered treadmill helped farmers grow more food.

1
Introduction

Water brings life to the earth, while the sun god T'ien shines over everyone—farmer, soldier, merchant, and rich man alike. You stand alongside your father, each of you running in place on a **bamboo** treadmill. Your uncle is in the field tending the rice crop and watching as your treadmill moves bamboo paddles in and out of the river. The faster you step, the more water flows into the rice fields. Your mother and sisters will cook rice tonight with a bit of seaweed and fish, and the whole family—sisters, brothers, parents, grandparents, cousins, aunts, and uncles—will gather.

Just like the boy on the treadmill, you can be productive while staying in one place. As you read this book you will take a journey through time to ancient China, where one of the earliest and most fascinating civilizations was born. You will travel back thousands of years to visit farmers, craftsmen, artists, inventors, nobles, and emperors. Through various activities and projects, you will learn about tools and discoveries, festivals and games, and the way of life from the earliest kingdoms to China's Golden Age.

Making silk from the threads of the silkworm cocoon takes patience, soft hands, and nimble fingers.

2
The Shang and Chou Dynasties: The Bronze Age

Some of the earliest people to settle in ancient China were the Yangshao and the Lungshan. They settled along riverbanks, growing grains and living in houses made of wood and earth. They made pottery from clay and discovered how to turn silkworm cocoons into thread and cloth. Very little is known about their everyday life, but as these early farmers handed down their knowledge, they helped later generations of Chinese develop useful and clever inventions long before the rest of the world.

Around 2000 BCE to 250 BCE, two ruling families, the Shang and the Chou, governed the vast land that is China. At the time, most Chinese were peasant farmers. They struggled to feed their families and worked endlessly in service to the rich **feudal lords**. Farmers, along with craftspeople and merchants, lived in humble villages. Nobles, warriors, and other important leaders lived inside walled cities. They enjoyed fine silk clothing, food, wine, hunting, and art. During this period the Chinese mastered the skill of melting copper, tin, and lead together to make bronze. Using this strong metal, craftsmen formed an array of tools, weapons, ceremonial objects, and utensils. Historians call this era the Bronze Age.

In ceremonies honoring their ancestors, the Chinese cooked with ornamental bronze pots such as this.

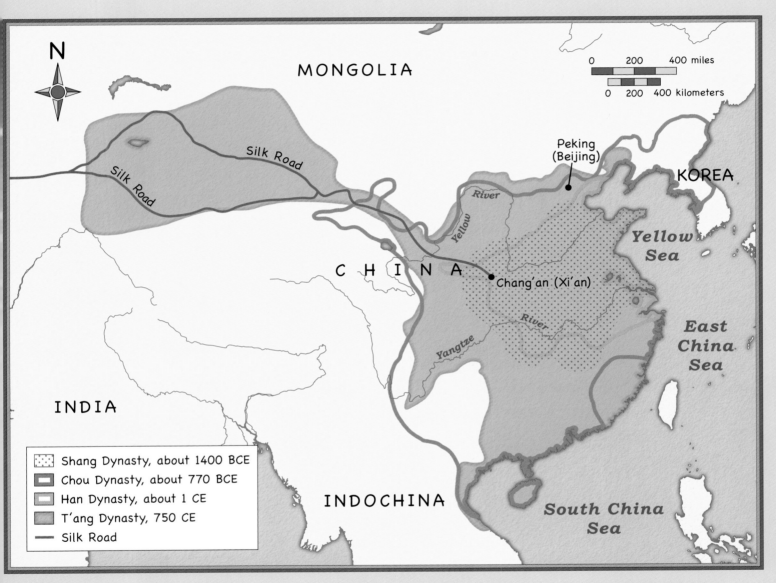

This map shows the vast overland trade routes and seaports used by the ancient Chinese to trade silk and other luxuries to Asia and Europe.

Bellows

It is winter, and it is dark, but it is not cold beside the giant oven where you and your uncles are casting bronze. To melt the metal, the ovens need to be very, very hot. You have just carried in another armload of wood. Your uncle adds the wood to the fire, and your father comes into the room with the bellows. "My son, you are strong," he says. "Take the bellows and pump as hard and fast as you can. Our fire will grow mighty." When you reach out for the bellows, your father is proud of your willingness to work hard. "We will be casting drinking cups today. I will let you choose how we decorate them. What shall it be? Tigers, dragons, sheep, rabbits, or birds?"

"Dragons," you say. "They breathe fire, just like us!"

You will need:

- a sturdy cardboard shipping box (about the shape and size of a shoe box)
- a wooden rod or dowel twice the length of the box
- glue
- scissors
- extra piece of sturdy cardboard
- metal thumbtack
- feathers
- packing tape
- pencil
- adult helper

---

1. Set the cardboard box on your work surface. The longer sides are the top and bottom, the shorter sides are the ends. Place one end of the dowel against the center of one of the ends of the box, and trace around it using the pencil.

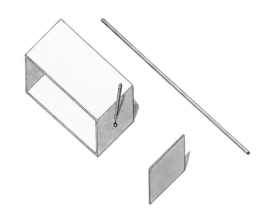

2. Carefully cut out the space you just traced, following the lines on the inside of your markings so that the opening will fit the dowel tightly.

3. Take the extra piece of cardboard and cut it to be the same size as the end of the box.

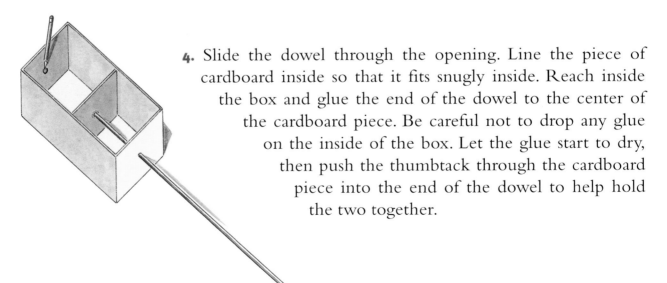

4. Slide the dowel through the opening. Line the piece of cardboard inside so that it fits snugly inside. Reach inside the box and glue the end of the dowel to the center of the cardboard piece. Be careful not to drop any glue on the inside of the box. Let the glue start to dry, then push the thumbtack through the cardboard piece into the end of the dowel to help hold the two together.

5. At the opposite side of the box, cut a $\frac{1}{2}$-by-$\frac{1}{2}$ inch hole in the center. Around the edges of the inside of the hole, glue bits of feathers.

6. Check to see that the dowel and cardboard can move easily, but tightly, back and forth inside the box. Then close the box, and seal all the seams with tape.

7. Now you have a Chinese box bellows. To test it, have an adult with you. Stand a safe distance from a small fire in a campsite or fireplace. Point the small opening of the bellows toward the fire, and pull the dowel in and out quickly. The bellows will take in air around the feathered opening, and the dowel and cardboard will push the air back out, fanning the fire.

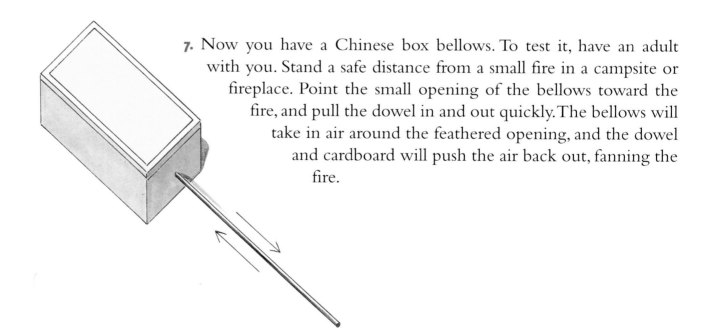

A Farmer's Home

When the great red gate opens, you can see inside the city's walls. Excitedly, you point out to your younger sister the palace of the feudal lord. Together, you admire the towering green door and the many windows with their painted yellow shutters. "Our lord is very powerful," you tell your sister. "For yellow is the color of the emperor."

"Yes," your sister sighs, "it is a grand house. But I like our house more because our father built it with good, rich earth. Besides, how could I not prefer our home? It is where our family lives!"

"And the spirits of our ancestors are there with us, too!" you add.

You will need:

- potter's clay
- scissors
- kitchen knife
- newspaper
- cardboard square
- Elmer's glue

- thread
- small sticks, twigs, or bamboo cooking skewers
- narrow leaves (fresh green ones are easiest to work with)

1. Spread newspaper on your work surface.

2. Cut or form the clay so that you can slice it into strips about ½ inch high and ½ inch across.

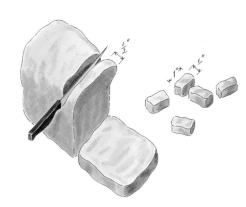

3. Then cut the strips of clay into blocks, about 1 inch long.

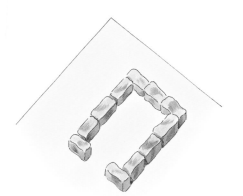

4. Use the cardboard as the ground that your building will sit on. Lay the blocks in a rectangle about 4 by 3 inches, and leave an opening for a door on one of the 3-inch walls. Stack the blocks on top of each other, making sure that the small spaces between the blocks do not line up.

5. After stacking three rows, leave a space on one or two walls for windows.

6. When your house is high enough, form an arch over the door opening, and stack blocks at the opposite wall in similar pattern. They should be the same height at the center.

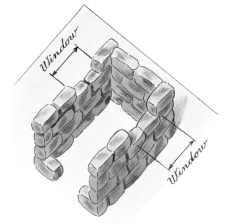

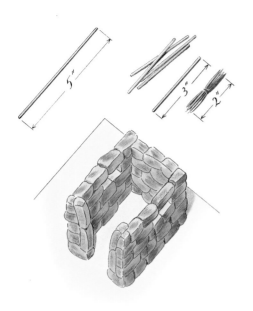

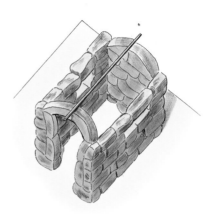

7. Cut a stick about 5 inches long. Lay the stick on top of the front door arch and the center of the back wall. Press lightly to keep it in place. This is your "ridge beam."

8. Cut sticks into 3-inch lengths.

9. Run a bead of Elmer's glue along the top of the ridge beam. Then lay each stick on the ridge beam and against a side wall. To make the roof frame, alternate the sticks from one side to the other.

10. To make the thatching, gather a few leaves together and tie them into a bundle with the thread. Make several bundles. Trim the thread, and cut the leaves of each bundle about 1 to 2 inches long. Starting at the edges, place a dab of glue on the roof frame and press the leaves against the frame. Layer the bundles up toward the ridge beam so that upper bundles overlap lower.

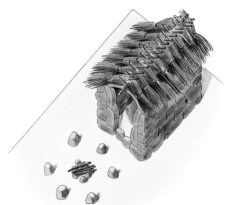

11. You house is done! Now you can build an entire village, if you like, but be sure all the doorways face East for good luck!

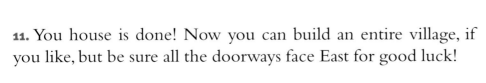

Bird of Joy Kite

You and your grandmother are gazing at distant hills when your grandmother smiles slowly and says, "Let me tell you the story of Mo Di, who lived on Lu Mountain."

You love those special times when your grandparents tell you stories, and so you nod eagerly and squat low on the ground. "Please, Grandmother," you say.

"Long ago, Mo Di, a great scientist and philosopher, believed he could make wood fly. For many days he carved a bird out of wood. He tied the bird to a string and took it up to the top of Lu Mountain. Sadly, after a single day, the bird fell out of the sky. But not long after, Lu Ban, a student of Mo Di, also tried to make a flying bird. Lu Ban used bamboo and silk. His kite flew joyfully in the sky for three days! Can you guess what kind of bird kite it was?" asked Grandmother with a wink.

"It was a magpie!" you exclaim. "Because the other name for magpie is bird of joy!"

You will need:

- strong kitchen scissors
- tissue or tracing paper
- fine nylon kite string
- plastic or lightweight fabric (optional)
- pencil
- two 12-inch bamboo cooking skewers
- black marker or paintbrush and black watercolor paint
- Elmer's glue
- ruler
- sewing needle (large eye)
- 1 inch by 24 inch (approximately) length of ripstop nylon or crepe paper

1. Snip off the pointed ends of the skewers with the scissors.

2. Position the scissors around each of the skewers, ¼ inch from each end. Twist each skewer inside the grip of the scissors to gouge out a notch in the bamboo.

3. Cut a piece of string about 6 inches longer than the length of one of the skewers. Tie one end of the string tightly around the end of a skewer so that it fits inside the notch. Then, make a loose knot and loop the string around the notch at the other end. Carefully tighten the knot around the notch, while, at the same time, pulling so that the skewer gently bends into a bow shape. Finish tying the knot, and trim excess string.

4. Next, lay the bowed skewer flat. Lay the other skewer over the center of the bowed skewer. Arrange the top skewer so that one-third of the skewer is above the bowed skewer and two-thirds of it below. Lash kite string around the skewers until they fit together tightly.

5. Cut a length of string 4 feet long. Tie a knot around the notch at the bottom of the kite. Make a small loop, and tie a knot to make it tight. You will use this loop later.

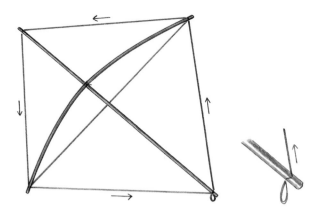

6. Run the rest of the string counterclockwise around the whole kite, stopping at each notch to tie a knot. Finish the kite frame by tying the string tightly around the bottom notch, and trim excess string.

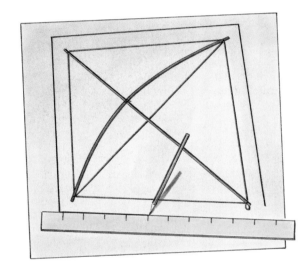

7. Lay your kite frame on the paper. Measure three quarters of an inch all the way around the kite frame and draw a pattern using the pencil. Cut it out.

8. Set your frame on the cutout. At each of the four pointed corners, snip off three quarters of an inch. Fold the edge of the paper three quarters of an inch over the top of the string of the frame. Glue the paper in place.

9. Flip the kite over and paint a magpie, "bird of joy," or any other bird on your kite.

10. Cut about 30 inches of string. Tie one end of this piece of string to the small loop you made at the bottom of the kite. Thread the other end through the eye of the needle. Poke the needle from the outside to the inside of the kite where the two crossbars meet. Leave 15 inches of string to dangle loosely on the finished side of the kite. On the inside, wrap the string several times around the intersection of the skewers and tie it tight. Cut excess string.

11. Pick up the 15 inches of string on the finished side, and raise the kite until the top lifts while the bottom is still lying flat. At this point in the string, tie a loop.

12. Now take your ball of kite string and tie it through the loop you have just made.

13. If you like, you may add lightweight tails to the bottom of your kite. To do so, tie the length of ripstop nylon or crepe paper around the skewer at the base of the kite.

14. When you are ready to fly the kite, turn the bowed skewer so that it pushes against the inside of the kite and curves. Now find a brisk wind and soar!

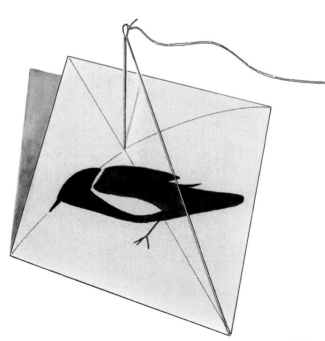

坑儒焚書

Emperor Qin Shi-huang disagreed with the teachings of Confucius, so he burned his books and punished students and scholars.

3

The Han Dynasty: The Classical Age

The last years of the Bronze Age were troublesome. Though the great thinker Kongfuzi (called "Confucius" in the West) was spreading his ideas about harmony and kindness, Chinese ruling families and their peasant armies were always fighting. Historians call the years 475-221 BCE the Warring States period. After much strife, one ruler united the people and became emperor. He was called Qin Shi-Huang, the "First Emperor." Qin is pronounced "Chin," and the word is thought to be the source of the name China. Though Qin's reign was short, he accomplished many things, including the building of the Great Wall. Unfortunately, he also burned the writings of Confucius.

After Qin's empire fell, the Han Dynasty came to power. During this era the Silk Road was established. This was an overland route between China and Europe that allowed China to trade with the Roman Empire. Europeans prized Chinese silk and they traded gold, ivory, gemstones, and glass for silk, jade, pottery, bronze, and lacquerware. During these prosperous times many festivals were created, and the government brought back the teachings of Confucius, which encouraged strong family ties and education for young boys. It was a time of great inventions, such as paper and ink, the wheelbarrow, the iron plow, the ship's **rudder**, and the hot-air balloon.

Some materials used in traditional Chinese papermaking are bamboo, hemp, silk, cloth rags, and mulberry bark.

Papermaking

You have always admired your grandfather's skill at **calligraphy**. He has a steady hand, and he knows how to draw thousands of **characters**. Some evenings he sits with you and reads to you from a vertical line of characters he has painted on strips of bamboo. "Grandfather," you say, "someday I hope to be as knowledgeable as you!"

"There is much to learn about this great world, my boy," says your grandfather. "You will go to school and learn from masters. You will study hard and work with mulberry paper and ink! You may become a teacher yourself! As Master Kungfuzi once said, 'All educated men are peers, or equals.'"

"Though I might become educated, Grandfather," you say, "I will never be your peer, but always your humble and devoted grandson!"

You will need:

- large bowl
- water
- two large sheets of newspaper or tissue paper
- washbasin
- electric blender
- measuring cup
- leaves, dried flowers, grass, thread (optional)
- plastic window screen (found at hardware stores)
- masking tape
- plastic stirring spoon
- felt
- sponge
- sunshine

1. Fill the bowl with warm water.

2. Shred the newspaper or tissue paper into small pieces, and place them in the bowl of water. Soak for about 30 minutes.

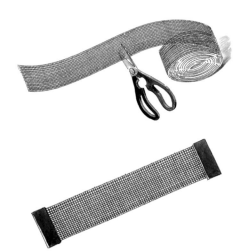

3. While the paper is soaking, prepare your screen. If you have an unfinished piece of screen, handle it carefully, to keep the frayed ends from poking you. Cut the screen to fit easily inside your basin. To make handles for the screen, fold over two opposite ends. Tape those edges.

4. Fill the blender with ½ cup water. Add twice that amount of soaked paper.

5. Run the blender on a medium-high speed. If it sounds like it is working too hard, add a bit more water. Do this for 30–40 seconds.

6. Fill the basin one-third of the way full with water. Add the paper pulp. Stir.

7 You may add decorative pieces at this point, such as leaves, flower petals, grass, or bits of thread.

8. Holding the screen at each end, set it in the basin, and making sure that the pulp is distributed evenly, guide the screen toward the bottom of the basin and then slowly raise it.

9. Let water drain from the screen. When it has stopped dripping, lay the piece of felt on top of the paper, and flip the two. Using the damp sponge, press on the back of the screen to force excess water out of the paper.

10. Slowly peel your sheet of paper off the screen. Let it dry in the sun on the felt.

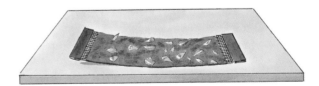

To celebrate holidays such as Chinese New Year, the Hungry Ghost festival, and the Harvest Moon, colorful lanterns are strung along streets, hung on bamboo poles, and placed over doorways.

Paper Lantern

Everyone is excited. The moon will be full tonight. It is the fifteenth day of the first **lunar month** of the year, the last night of the Chinese New Year celebration. You and your mother, grandmother, aunts, cousins, and sisters are happily making rice dumplings for the festival. You are teasing and joking with one another as you cook. "Our sweet Grandmother is making sweet rice balls with walnuts and rose petals." You laugh and turn to your sister. "You must be salty . . . your rice balls are filled with vegetables!"

"No matter," says your aunt. "Whether sweet or salty, a sticky rice dumpling is a sign of family unity, harmony, and happiness. Tonight we will be together to watch the lanterns as they are lit. We are blessed, and the year is young and full of promise!"

You will need:

- a sheet of heavy paper (construction paper, card stock, or presentation paper)
- decorative paper such as foil, colored tissue, or wrapping paper
- glue stick
- glitter and/or sequins (optional)
- colored markers (optional)
- scissors
- embroidery thread or yarn
- tape
- ruler
- pencil

1. Measure 1 inch from the short end of your heavy paper. Mark it with the pencil, and cut along the line. Set it aside.

2. Lay your heavy paper flat. Compose a design. Traditional lantern festival designs are birds, fish, tigers, or dragons. Glue the decorative pieces of paper and/or glitter and sequins to your design. Use color markers to draw on your lantern, if you wish.

3. Using the ruler, measure 1 inch from the edge of each of the long sides of the paper. Draw a line. This is your "do not cut" line.

4. Fold the paper lengthwise.

5. Using the ruler and pencil, start at one of the short edges and measure 1 inch and mark it. Continue marking off 1 inch until you reach the opposite side of the paper.

6. Start at the fold and cut on the first 1-inch mark up to the "do not cut" line. Do the same across the page.

7. Unfold the paper. Curve the sheet around so that the short edges are touching. Overlap one over the other, and tape or glue them together.

8. Take the strip of paper that you set aside and tape or glue it to the top of your lantern to form a handle.

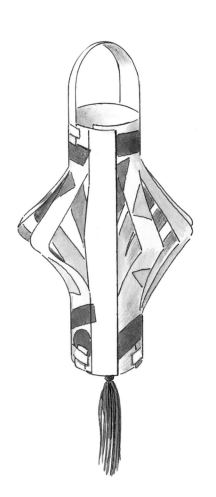

9. To make a tassel for the bottom of your lantern, cut several pieces of yarn or thread, each about 6 inches long. Cut an additional length of yarn or thread slightly longer than the diameter of your lantern. Lay the yarn flat and place the center of the tassel pieces on the center of the length of yarn. Bring the ends of the length of yarn or thread together and tie a knot around the tassel pieces. Suspend the tassel across the bottom of the lantern, keeping it centered. Tape one end of the yarn or thread tight. Tape the other end inside the lantern. Make a number of lanterns, string them together and decorate the night!

Playing Jianzi

You and your brother are walking past the market, and you see several groups of merchants at their stalls playing games with dice, tiles, or bamboo cards. After you buy supplies for school, you walk home along the river. "Look," says your brother, eyeing a group of men playing with a colorful set of cards. "Those men have cards made of paper!"

"Yes," you say, "I have seen the new paper cards before. They look fun, but I have no time to play. I must study."

"I love to play games, especially **jianzi** (say jon-zoo) and I want to learn to play many more games! Do you think I am lazy?" asks your brother with a grin.

"Not really," you say. "Even Master Kungfuzi says people should be able to play games. Didn't he tell his students that 'playing these games is better than being idle'?"

"Let's not be idle, then," laughs your brother. "Let's hurry home and play jianzi!"

You will need:

- two corks
- four feathers, 12 inches long
- Elmer's glue
- string
- scissors
- lightweight fabric, about 7 by 7 inches
- corkscrew or awl
- adult helper

1. Ask an adult to help you pierce two holes in each cork, using a corkscrew or an awl.

2. Insert one or two feathers in each hole.

3. Place a small dab of glue in the holes around each feather, and coat the bottom side of each cork with glue to add weight and balance. Let dry.

4. Lay the fabric on a work surface, and center the corks and feathers side by side.

5. Cut a piece of string about 8 inches long.

6. Gather up the fabric and tie the string tightly, around the base of the feathers, just above the top of the corks. You may want to wrap and tie the string a few times for added strength. Trim the string and any long flaps of fabric.

7. Now find a partner or form a team, and keep the jianzi in the air with only your feet.

Confucius is the most well known of Chinese philosophers. His teachings were about love, honoring one's parents, the value of education, and treating one another with respect.

4

The T'ang Dynasty: The Golden Age

Several dynasties ruled China after the Han Dynasty and there was much fighting and bloodshed. The Chinese invented gunpowder and because this made weapons more powerful, enemy armies held off and the battles quieted. In 618 CE the T'ang Dynasty came to power, and peace and prosperity fell over the land. Three important religions gave people spiritual guidance: **Confucianism**, **Taoism**, and **Buddhism**. The T'ang ruler was very open-minded. He built a new capital city, called Ch'ang-an, meaning "long-lasting peace." Nearly two million people moved to the new city. It was a great cultural center. People flocked to performances of opera, music, theater, and dance. The fine arts—especially painting, calligraphy, and poetry—were highly valued.

Trade with the West brought an exchange of goods and new ideas. The Chinese were the first in the world to make paper and to print books. They had developed fine oceangoing ships, called **junks**, that had special sails, rudders for steering, and a mariner's **compass** for direction. Trade brought an exciting exchange of foods. The Chinese quickly added new flavors to their *fan ts'ai* way of cooking with foods and spices such as garlic, spinach, bananas, mustard, grapes, and sugar. Today, the world looks upon the T'ang Dynasty as China's Golden Age.

Oceangoing Chinese junks return to busy Shanghai harbor to unload cargoes of spice and other trade goods.

Mariner's Compass

You spy your father's ship in the harbor. He is a junk captain, and his great ship left laden with pottery. He has returned with sweet-smelling spices, such as mace, nutmeg, and cloves. Your father has a compass aboard, and this helps him find his way to and from the exotic lands across the South China Sea faster than anyone else.

You rush to the docks. It is noisy and crowded. Men everywhere are loading and unloading cargo. It is exciting and confusing all at the same time. But your father sees you and waves. "Father," you cry, "welcome home!"

You want to ask, "Have you brought me a gift?" But you know that is impolite. Your father greets you and, with a smile, hands you a cloth bag. You quickly open the bag, and a dozen bright orange balls fall out. "Father," you ask, "what have you brought me? What are these strange round things?"

Your father picks one up and takes out his knife. As he slowly cuts into it the air fills with the most unbelievable perfume. "Taste," says your father, handing you a small, juicy slice.

"Heaven!" you say.

"No," says your father, "tangerine."

You will need:

- small bowl
- sheet of paper
- sewing needle (about 1 inch)
- pen
- scissors
- Scotch tape
- cork
- kitchen knife
- cutting board
- water
- magnet
- ruler
- hammer (optional)
- adult helper

1. Set out the sheet of paper. Place the bowl upside down on the paper and trace it.

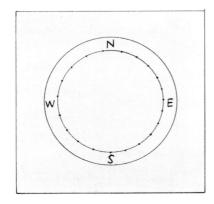

2. With the ruler, measure ½ inch in from the circle. Make a small dot with the marker. Do this several times around the circle. Connect the dots to make an inner circle. Using the marker, write an N (North) in between the lines. Directly across from the N, write an S (South). To the right of the N, write an E (East), and across from the E, write a W (West).

3. Cut out the larger circle. Then cut out the inner circle, so that you are left with a ring with the letters N, E, S, W. Tape this ring to the lip of your bowl.

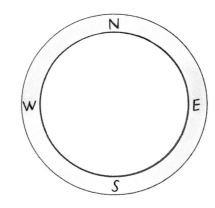

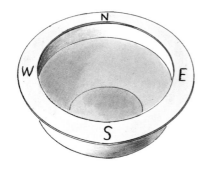

4. Fill the bowl three-quarters full with water.

5. With the help of an adult, set the cork on a cutting board and slice a small circle off one end. Then cut this circle in half to make a semicircle.

6. Take the needle and rub it in ONE direction across the magnet. Do this several times.

7. Carefully spear the needle through the cork so that an equal amount of needle shows on both sides of the cork. If you need help pushing the needle, tap it gently with a small hammer.

8. Set the bowl outside or near a window. Using what you know about where you are, place the bowl so that the N points North. If you do not know where North is, then place the bowl so that the W points toward where the sun sets.

9. Put the needle in the bowl of water. To make certain that the needle floats flat on the surface of the water be sure that the needle is centered through the middle of the cork. Slowly, the needle will turn toward the pole closest to you, either North or South. (In ancient China, mariner's compasses pointed to the South).

Chinese printmakers were the first to use India ink, a permanent ink made from pine soot and lamp oils.

Block Printing

You are nervous. Today you study. Your grandparents marvel at your books, with poems and paintings on sheets of paper. Until you began your studies, no one in your family had ever seen a printed book before. You are grateful that your parents allowed you to attend school. Tomorrow you will go to the examination hall, along with thousands of other boys. Locked in your cell, you will take your civil service examination. "Oh, to be chosen," you sigh. If you do well, you will be given an honorable position in the government. Your family will not go wanting again. But today you open your books and prepare.

You will need:

- a block of wood
- printer's ink or liquid tempera paint
- scissors
- paintbrush
- craft foam (available at craft stores, or ask at the meat counter of your local grocery store for clean meat trays)
- tacky glue
- blank paper
- Scotch tape

1. On a plain sheet of paper, draw your design, such as dragon, **pagoda,** panda, or tiger. Cut it out.

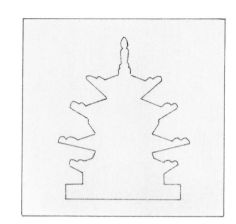

2. Tape the design to a piece of craft foam. Now cut the design into the craft foam.

3. Glue the craft foam to the wood, and wait until it dries.

4. Prepare your ink or paint. Dip your brush into the paint, and paint your foam. Be careful not to drip ink or paint onto the block.

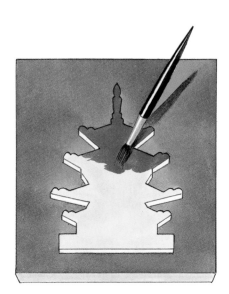

5. Set your paper over the foam and, using your flattened palms, press down. If you want to make multiple prints, you will need to repaint the foam each time. You can make several different designs or make a pattern.

Egg Drop Soup

The family has come together for the midday meal, as always. You sit with your grandparents, parents, brothers, and sisters around the table, where all the food is set in the middle. All of you will share food from the same bowls. Each of you has a pair of chopsticks and a small porcelain spoon. Everyone allows your grandparents to begin eating first, then your parents, and finally the children. "Honor your elders!" your mother always says. You can hardly wait to eat. One of your favorite foods is being served; egg drop soup. But you keep that a secret, as you have always been told, "Children must never have favorites; they must eat equal amounts of everything!" But you savor every spoonful of soup!

A meal is often called *fan ts'ai*. *Fan* means "grain," such as rice, wheat, or millet. *Ts'ai* means "side dishes." Because of the Silk Road trade, the Chinese eagerly tried new foods and spices and added them to their side dishes. They cut their food into tiny pieces, to blend the flavors. Also, because there are few forests, there was little wood for cooking. People didn't want to waste fuel, so they cooked the side dishes quickly, usually by boiling, steaming, or frying in very hot oil.

You will need:

- one-quart stockpot
- small mixing bowl
- measuring cup
- measuring spoons
- fork
- wire whisk
- 2 cups chicken broth

- 1 egg
- 1 teaspoon salt
- 1 teaspoon cornstarch
- 2 tablespoons cold water
- 3 spinach leaves
- kitchen scissors
- adult helper

1. Add the salt to the chicken broth. With an adult's help, heat on a medium–high setting until it boils.

2. While the chicken broth is heating up, wash the spinach and use the scissors to cut the leaves into narrow strips. Set aside.

3. Mix the cornstarch and cold water in a bowl. This will make a thickening paste.

4. Add the paste mixture to the broth, and stir. Let the broth boil again.

5. In the measuring cup, stir the egg with the fork (gently, so that bubbles do not form).

6. Turn off the heat.

7. Hold the measuring cup with the egg about 8 inches above the stockpot. Slowly pour the egg into the pot. At the same time, stir the soup in one direction with the wire whisk.

8. Add the strips of spinach to your soup. Let the leaves soften.

9. Eat hearty! And remember, it is all right to slurp!

Glossary

bamboo: A large, woody grass used in construction and in making furniture, tools, utensils, and other household items.

Buddhism: Religious faith based on the teachings of Buddha, an Indian holy man.

calligraphy: Decorative writing.

Chinese characters: Symbols representing images, sounds, and concepts that are used to express words and ideas in the Chinese language.

compass: A device that gives geographic direction, by using a magnetized needle that points toward the earth's magnetic poles.

Confucianism: Faith in the ideas of Confucius, who believed in the importance of family, ancestor worship, and education.

fan ts'ai: A traditional Chinese meal. The main dish is *fan*, or grain, such as millet or corn or rice, served with *ts'ai*, or side dishes, such as meat, vegetables, or eggs.

feudal lords: Wealthy nobles owning the land that peasants farm.

jianzi: (Say jon-zoo) a game played like Hacky Sack.

junks: Chinese boats designed with special sails, rudders, and compass.

lunar month: The period of time between the new moon and the full moon.

pagoda: A towerlike building with decorative rooflines that is usually a temple or shrine.

rudder: A device used to steer a boat.

Taoism: A religious faith that believes in living a simple life in harmony with nature.

Metric Conversion Chart

You can use the chart below to convert from U. S. measurements to the metric system.

Weight
1 ounce = 28 grams
½ pound (8 ounces) = 227 grams
1 pound = .45 kilogram
2.2 pounds = 1 kilogram

Liquid volume
1 teaspoon = 5 milliliters
1 tablespoon = 15 milliliters
1 fluid ounce = 30 milliliters
1 cup = 240 milliliters (.24 liter)
1 pint = 480 milliliters (.48 liter)
1 quart = .95 liter

Length
¼ inch = .6 centimeter
½ inch = 1.25 centimeters
1 inch = 2.5 centimeters

Temperature
100°F = 40°C
110°F = 45°C
350°F = 180°C
375°F = 190°C
400°F = 200°C
425°F = 220°C
450°F = 235°C

About the Author

Ruth Bjorklund is a former children's librarian who has written several nonfiction books for young people. She lives on Bainbridge Island in Washington State, and especially loves to take her family by ferry into Seattle's International District, to enjoy dim sum, a Chinese meal that means "heart's delight."

Find Out More

Books

Cotterell Arthur. *Ancient China*. New York: Knopf, 1994.

Krasno, Rena. *Cloud Weavers: Ancient Chinese Legends*. Berkeley, CA: Pacific View Press, 2002.

O'Connor, Jane. *The Emperor's Silent Army: Terracotta Warriors of Ancient China*. New York: Viking, 2002.

Pilegard, Virginia Walton. *The Warlord's Kites*. Gretna, LA: Pelican Publishing, 2004.

Rainey, Rhonda. *Papermaking for the First Time*. New York: Sterling Publishing, 2002.

Williams, Brian. *Ancient China*. New York: Viking, 1996.

Web Sites

Ancient China
http://www.historylink101.com/china_history.htm

China's Science and Technology
http://www.crystalinks.com/chinascience.html

Chinese Inventions
http://www.computersmiths.com/chineseinvention/index.html

Daily Life in Ancient China
http://members.aol.com/Donnclass/Chinalife.html

Index